I. Introduction

The rate of increase in labor productivity — an essential element determining improvements in living standards — slowed in the mid-2000s, as highlighted by Fernald (2012), Gordon (2012), Jorgenson (2012), and Kahn and Rich (2013), among others. If this development persists, the long-run outlook for economic growth, and for improvements in living standards, will have darkened. Accordingly, it is important to identify the source of the slowdown and assess the implications for future growth.

One possible explanation of the slow pace of growth is that the economy has taken a long time to recover from the financial crisis and Great Recession, as the repair of balance sheets has proceeded slowly and as uncertainty about the pace of the recovery has held back investment.[1] Although the slowdown in labor productivity growth started before the onset of the financial crisis, those developments could, nonetheless, be contributing to the continued tepid advance. Another possibility — advocated most prominently by Cowen (2011) — is that the U.S. economy has entered a long period of stagnation as the easy innovations largely have been exploited already. Gordon (2012, 2013) has offered a third take on the slowdown, related to Cowen's. Namely, Gordon argues that the information technology revolution has mostly run its course and that the boost to productivity growth in the mid-1990s from those developments lasted only about a decade.[2] Brynjolfsson and McAfee (2011) and others have made the opposite argument, that the information technology (IT) revolution still has a long way to run and will

---

[1] Reinhart and Rogoff (2009) documented the typical pattern of slow recovery from financial crises. See Fernald (2012) for a discussion of the performance of productivity before, during, and after the Great Recession.

[2] A large literature has examined these issues in the past. For our contribution to this literature and for citations to the earlier literature, see Oliner and Sichel (2000, 2002) and Oliner, Sichel, and Stiroh (2007). An interesting recent paper is Feenstra, Mandel, Reinsdorf, and Slaughter (2013). They present evidence that about one-eighth of the pickup in labor productivity growth in the United States (and one-fifth of the pickup in multifactor productivity growth) after 1995 reflected mismeasurement in the terms of trade.

continue to dramatically transform the U.S. economy.[3] Taking a middle ground, Baily, Manyika, and Gupta (2013) argue that technology (in IT or other fields) is not stagnating but that the future path of productivity is very uncertain. The question raised by this debate is the central focus of this paper: Is the IT revolution in the United States over?[4]

Obviously, this question is difficult to answer. The structural transformations and economic benefits spawned by continuing advances in IT are challenging to track and quantify. For example, what will be the economic consequences of massively greater connectivity with handheld and other devices and ready access to huge amounts of information, of 3-D printing and other dramatic changes in manufacturing processes, and of the changes brought on by companies like Google, Apple, Facebook, and Amazon that have rapidly come to dominate market segments that were not even imagined some years ago? One way to cut through this complexity is to concentrate on a central theme in these developments — the ability to harness ever-greater computing power that comes in progressively smaller and less expensive packages. That focus on the capital that lies behind the IT revolution drives the analysis in this paper. Our analysis is by no means definitive, but we believe it provides a useful contribution to the debate over whether the IT revolution is over.

Our evidence comes in three parts. First, we use the growth accounting framework developed by Oliner and Sichel (2002) and Oliner, Sichel, and Stiroh (2007) to assess the contribution of IT to growth in labor productivity. This methodology is well suited to the task because it focuses on the contribution of IT to labor productivity growth from both the *use* of IT

---

[3] We use the term IT to refer to the collection of technologies related to computer hardware, software, and communication equipment. Other authors have used the term ICT (referring to information and communication technologies). We regard the two terms as synonymous. Although the IT capital considered in this paper encompasses a wide range of assets, it excludes intangible capital other than software. For research that takes intangible capital into account, see Corrado, Hulten, and Sichel (2009), Corrado and Hulten (2012), Corrado, Haskel, Jona-Lasinio, and Iommi (2012), and Oliner, Sichel, and Stiroh (2007).

[4] For more on Brynjolfsson's and Gordon's perspectives, see their debate on TED (Technology, Entertainment, Design) on February 26, 2013. Available at http://conferences.ted.com/TED2013/program/guide.php.

and from efficiency gains in the **production** of IT and because it can be updated with the most recent data to provide estimates through 2012. Our growth accounting evidence indicates that the contribution of IT to labor productivity growth in the United States from 2004 to 2012 stepped down to roughly its contribution from the mid-1970s to 1995. This evidence supports the view that the contribution from IT is no longer providing the boost to growth in labor productivity that it did during the years of the productivity resurgence from 1995 to 2004. Nonetheless, the IT contribution remains substantial, accounting for more than a third of labor productivity growth since 2004.

Those results indicate where the economy has been. For the second part of our answer, we use the steady state of our multi-sector growth model to assess the outlook for growth in labor productivity. This part of the paper allows us to translate alternative assumptions about the pace of technological progress in the IT sector and the rest of the economy into an overall growth rate of labor productivity. We find that a plausible assessment of these underlying trends points to labor productivity growth of 1.8 percent annually. This projection is about the same as the average forecast of other productivity analysts.

Our baseline projection represents a modest pickup from the sluggish pace of labor productivity growth experienced since 2004. The pickup reflects ongoing advances in IT and an assumption that those gains and innovations in other sectors spur some improvement in multifactor productivity (MFP) growth outside of the IT sector relative to its tepid pace from 2004 to 2012.[5] These developments feed through the economy to provide a modest boost to labor productivity growth. That said, our projection of growth in labor productivity falls short of

---

[5] See Baily,Manyika, and Gupta (2013) for a discussion of ongoing innovation in different sectors of the economy.

the long-run average rate of 2¼ percent that has prevailed since 1889 and suggests neither a return to rapid growth nor economic stagnation but rather a period of moderate gains.[6]

Given the ongoing advance in semiconductor technology described below, along with the uneven pattern of productivity growth during earlier epochs of innovation, we also consider an alternative scenario in which a somewhat faster pace of improvement in IT spurs more rapid innovation throughout the economy.[7] With plausible assumptions, this alternative scenario generates labor productivity growth of about 2½ percent, above the long-run historical average.

Finally, we reassess the pace of advance of semiconductor technology.[8] We believe that these developments are an essential consideration, because exceptionally rapid improvements in semiconductor technology — making computing power faster, smaller, and cheaper — have been a key ingredient of the IT revolution. On this front, the official price indexes for semiconductors developed by the Bureau of Labor Statistics (BLS) show that quality-adjusted semiconductor prices are not falling nearly as rapidly as they did prior to the mid-2000s. This development implies, all else equal, that the pace of technical progress in the semiconductor industry has slowed, a narrative that would comport well with Gordon's view that the IT revolution in the United States largely is over. However, our reassessment indicates that technical progress in the semiconductor industry has continued to proceed at a rapid pace. We also provide preliminary results from a separate research project that suggest the BLS price series may have substantially understated the decline in semiconductor prices in recent years.

---

[6] To calculate this long historical average, we used data on output and hours from Kendrick (1961) for 1889-1929 and from the Bureau of Economic Analysis (output) and Kendrick (hours) for 1929-47. Gordon (2010, p. 25) provides details about the sources of these data series. For 1947-2012, we used data from the Bureau of Labor Statistics on output per hour in the nonfarm business sector. The growth rate over each period is calculated as the average log difference between the initial and final year of the period.

[7] As Chad Syverson points out in his comments on this paper, electrification generated, after a long lag, a period of elevated growth in labor productivity that lasted for about a decade. That pickup was followed by a slowdown in growth rates, but, subsequently, growth picked up again.

[8] For discussion of the linkages between the pace of innovation in semiconductor manufacturing and semiconductor prices, see Aizcorbe, Oliner, and Sichel (2008) and Flamm (2007).

Our three types of analysis, taken together, provide some useful insights into the question of whether the IT revolution is over. While the growth accounting evidence through 2012 confirms Gordon's view that the contribution from IT has fallen since 2004, the results from our steady-state analysis and our evidence on semiconductor prices point in a more optimistic direction. To answer the question posed in the title of the paper: "No, we do not believe the IT revolution is over." While our baseline projection anticipates a period of slightly subpar gains for labor productivity, we see a reasonable prospect that the pace of labor productivity growth could rise back up to its long-run average of 2¼ percent or even move higher.

II. Growth Accounting: Analytical Framework, Data, and Results

This section assesses the contributions to the increase in labor productivity from 1974 to 2012 through the lens of a growth accounting model designed to focus on the use and production of IT capital.

A. Analytical Framework

Here we provide a brief overview of the growth accounting framework. Additional detail can be found in Oliner, Sichel, and Stiroh (2007), henceforth OSS, and the appendix to that paper.

The model that underlies our analysis differs from that in OSS only with regard to the treatment of intangible capital. Here, we use the measure of nonfarm business output in the National Income and Product Accounts (NIPAs), which excludes most types of intangible capital other than software. In contrast, OSS incorporated a broader set of intangible assets to explore the role of intangibles in driving productivity growth. Although that analysis yielded useful insights about the sources of growth, the standard output measure used here lines up with the official data for the United States.

The growth accounting model divides nonfarm business into four sectors that produce final output: computer hardware, software, communication equipment, and a large non-IT-producing sector. We also include a sector that produces semiconductors, which are either consumed as intermediate input by the domestic final-output sectors or exported. Every sector is assumed to have constant returns to scale, and we assume the economy is perfectly competitive. In addition, as discussed in OSS, we allow for cyclical variation in the utilization of capital and labor and for adjustment costs that reduce market output when firms install new capital. The treatment of both adjustment costs and cyclical utilization follows that in Basu, Fernald, and Shapiro (2001).

The appendix to OSS shows that this model generates a standard decomposition of growth in output per hour:

(1) $$\dot{Y} - \dot{H} = \sum_j \alpha_j^K \left(\dot{K}_j - \dot{H} \right) + \alpha^L \dot{q} + M\dot{F}P,$$

where the dots signify growth rates; Y is nonfarm business output; H is aggregate hours worked; K_j is capital input of type j (where j = computer hardware, software, communication equipment, and an aggregate of all other tangible capital); α^L and α_j^K are, respectively, the income shares for labor and each type of capital; q measures labor composition effects that create a wedge between aggregate labor input and hours worked; and MFP denotes multifactor productivity. Equation 1 expresses the growth in labor productivity as the sum of the contributions from capital deepening, compositional changes in labor input, and multifactor productivity.[9]

---

[9] Equation 1 simplifies one aspect of the expression derived in OSS. Technically, the weight on the capital deepening term for type j capital equals its income share minus the elasticity of adjustment costs with respect to that type of capital. We have suppressed the adjustment cost elasticity in equation 1. Because empirical estimates of asset-specific adjustment cost elasticities are not available, OSS approximated the theoretically correct weights with standard income shares. We do the same here and simply start from that point in equation 1. The approximation does not affect the total weight summed across the capital terms, as the theoretically correct weights and the standard capital income shares both sum to one minus the labor share. But the approximation could result in some misallocation of the weights across types of capital.

The other key result from the model is an expression for the decomposition of aggregate MFP growth into sectoral contributions:

$$(2) \qquad \dot{MFP} = \sum_i \mu_i \dot{MFP}_i + \mu_S \dot{MFP}_S,$$

where i indexes the final-output sectors (computer hardware, software, communication equipment, and all other nonfarm business); S denotes the semiconductor sector; and each μ represents gross output in that sector divided by aggregate value added, both in current dollars. Thus, aggregate MFP growth equals a share-weighted sum of the sectoral MFP growth rates. We estimate these sectoral growth rates with the "dual" method that employs data on prices of output and inputs, rather than data on quantities. Because the necessary price data are available much sooner than the corresponding quantity data, the dual method allows us to calculate more timely estimates of sectoral MFP growth.

B. Data

For the most part, the data sources track those used in OSS and Oliner and Sichel (2000, 2002), which relied heavily on data from the BLS and the NIPAs. That said, we have made some changes to our data sources. We highlight briefly a few key changes here, with details on our data sources provided in an appendix.

For our capital deepening estimates, we are now working from a higher level of aggregation than in our earlier research. Previously, we built up estimates of capital deepening from data on 63 different types of assets, including detail on different types of hardware and software. Now, for the period from 1987 to 2010 for which the BLS provides extensive data, we are starting directly with BLS estimates for hardware, software, and communication equipment; that is, we are using the BLS aggregation within these categories rather than doing our own aggregation. Similarly, we are relying directly on BLS data for estimates of overall capital deepening. For 2011 and 2012 we extend the BLS data using NIPA data at this higher level of aggregation. Before 1987, the BLS does not provide the necessary detail for IT capital on its website, and we splice in estimates from the data constructed in OSS.

For the decomposition of MFP growth into sectoral contributions, we now use different price indexes for the output of the communications sector and the semiconductor sector. For the communications sector, we use the price index developed by Byrne and Corrado (2007), which falls more rapidly than does the NIPA price index for communication equipment. For semiconductor prices, we use the new index developed for the Federal Reserve's Industrial Production data.[10] The Fed's series incorporates a new hedonic index for microprocessors (MPUs) since 2006 that falls more rapidly than the current BLS price index.

C. Results

Table 1 summarizes our growth accounting results, both for the decomposition of labor productivity growth into capital deepening and aggregate MFP (to highlight IT use) and for the decomposition of MFP growth (to highlight efficiency gains in IT production).

As can be seen from the first three columns, labor productivity growth during 2004 to 2012 ran at just above an annual rate of 1½ percent, down considerably from the elevated pace during 1995 to 2004 and in line with the disappointing average rate that prevailed over the prior two decades. The sources of labor productivity growth follow a similar pattern, with both the contribution of overall capital deepening and MFP growth coming back down over 2004-2012 to about the pace observed from 1974 to 1995.

The memo item in the table shows the combined contribution to labor productivity growth from the **use** and ***production*** of IT. That contribution was 0.64 percentage point from 2004 to 2012, down significantly from its value from 1995 to 2004 and even a little below its

---

[10] This index was incorporated into the Industrial Production data in March 2013.

contribution from 1974 to 1995. Nonetheless, the contribution of IT to labor productivity growth remains sizable, accounting for more than one-third of the growth in labor productivity from 2004 to 2012. The substantial contribution of IT is notable given that the share of total income accruing to IT capital remains small and that the IT-producing sector has never accounted for as much as 7 percent of current-dollar output in nonfarm business (figure 1).

As for the separate contributions from the use of IT (capital deepening) and from efficiency gains in the production of IT, the patterns are similar, with the contributions over 2004-2012 well off from the rapid pace during 1995-2004 and a little below the contribution from 1974 to 1995. The slowdown in the contribution from the production of IT reflects both a slower pace of advance of MFP in each IT sector and a sizable step-down in the current-dollar output share of the industries producing computer hardware, communication equipment, and semiconductors. This drop reflects substantial movement of IT manufacturing from the United States to foreign locations. Indeed, as shown in figure 1, the share of current-dollar nonfarm business output represented by the production of computer hardware, communication equipment, and semiconductors has fallen more than 70 percent from its peak in 2000.[11] In contrast, the output share of the software industry was higher from 2004 to 2012 than in either of the earlier periods.

These estimates reinforce Gordon's story that the contribution of the IT revolution has been disappointing since the mid-2000s. That said, sorting out the implications of these results for the future role of IT in the U.S. economy is difficult. One possibility is that the IT revolution largely has run its course and will provide much less of a lasting imprint on living standards than did the earlier epochs of innovation. Another possibility is that the boost to labor productivity

---

[11] As discussed later in the paper, these shares likely are understated because the domestic activity of these firms is mismeasured to some extent. However, correcting any such mismeasurement would leave the trends in figure 1 intact.

growth is taking a pause during the transition from the PC era to the post-PC era. Just as a long lag transpired from the development of the PC in the early 1980s to the subsequent pickup in labor productivity growth, there could be a lagged payoff from the development and diffusion of extensive connectivity, handheld devices, and ever-greater and cheaper computing power.

In 1987, Robert Solow famously said "You see the computer revolution everywhere except in the productivity data."[12] As highlighted by Oliner and Sichel (1994), computers comprised too small a share of the capital stock in 1987 to have made a large contribution to overall productivity growth. But, several years later, the imprint of the revolution became very evident. In a parallel vein, one could now say: "You see massive connectivity and ever-cheaper computing power everywhere but in the productivity data." Subsequently, those contributions could become evident in aggregate data. That, of course, is just speculation about the future. The next part of our analysis looks ahead to highlight plausible paths for labor productivity growth in the years ahead.

III. Outlook for Productivity Growth

We now turn to the outlook for labor productivity in the United States. The first part of this section uses the steady state of our growth accounting model to develop estimates of future growth of labor productivity. We then compare the steady-state results to the projections from a variety of other sources.

A. Steady-state Analysis

We update the steady-state analysis in Oliner and Sichel (2002) and OSS to incorporate the latest available data. As in that earlier work, we impose a set of conditions on the growth accounting model to derive an expression for the growth of labor productivity in the steady state.

---

[12] "We'd Better Watch Out." *New York Times Book Review*, July 12, p. 36

These conditions include that (i) real output in each sector grows at a constant rate (which differs across sectors); (ii) real investment in each type of capital grows at the same constant rate as the real stock of that capital; (iii) labor hours grow at the same constant rate in every sector; (iv) the workweek is constant; and (v) the growth contribution from the change in labor composition is constant.

Under these conditions, the appendix to OSS shows that the steady-state growth of aggregate labor productivity can be expressed as:

$$(3) \qquad \dot{Y} - \dot{H} = \sum_i \left[\left(\alpha_i^K / \alpha^L \right) \left(M\dot{F}P_i + \beta_i^S M\dot{F}P_S \right) \right] + \dot{q} + M\dot{F}P,$$

with

$$(4) \qquad M\dot{F}P = \sum_i \mu_i M\dot{F}P_i + \mu_S M\dot{F}P_S.$$

As before, the α's denote income shares for each type of capital, β_i^S is the semiconductor share of total costs in final-output sector i, $\dot{q}$ is the change in labor composition, and the μ's denote current-dollar output shares in each sector. The expression for aggregate MFP growth in equation 4 is unchanged from equation 2, the expression that holds outside the steady state. Although no explicit terms for capital deepening appear in equation 3, capital deepening is determined endogenously from the improvement in technology. The terms in brackets capture the growth contribution from this induced capital deepening. Accordingly, equation 3 shows that steady-state growth in output per hour equals the sum of growth in MFP, the change in labor composition, and the contribution from the capital deepening induced by MFP growth.[13]

Steady-state growth in labor productivity depends on a large number of parameters — about 30 in all after accounting for those that lie behind the income shares and sectoral MFP

_____

[13]In the steady state, cyclical factors and adjustment costs have no effect on MFP growth. These effects disappear as a consequence of assuming that the workweek is constant and that investment and capital stock grow at the same rate for each type of capital.

growth rates shown in equations 3 and 4. We consider a range of values for these parameters. The complete list can be found in appendix table A1. Individually, most of these parameters do not have large effects on the steady-state growth rate. However, two parameters in equations 3 and 4 are important: the rate of improvement in labor composition and MFP growth for nonfarm business outside the IT-producing sector ("other nonfarm business"). For labor composition effects, we rely on the latest projection based on the methodology in Jorgenson, Ho, and Stiroh (2005).[14] In this projection, changes in labor composition boost labor productivity growth only 0.07 percentage point per year on average between 2012 and 2022, as educational attainment is anticipated to reach a plateau. To allow for uncertainty around this projection, we specify a range that runs from 0 to 0.14 percentage point. For MFP growth in other nonfarm business, we use values that range from 0.06 to 0.62 percent per year. The lower bound equals the average growth rate from 2004 to 2012, while the upper bound equals two-thirds of the much faster pace registered from the mid-1990s to 2004, which would be a notable improvement over the recent performance.[15]

Using equations 3 and 4, we find that steady-state growth in labor productivity ranges from an annual rate of 0.88 percent (when each parameter is set to its lower-bound value) to 2.82 percent (using the upper-bound values). The wide range reflects the uncertainty about the future values of the underlying parameters. To obtain a baseline steady-state estimate, we set each parameter to the midpoint of its range. The resulting estimate of 1.80 percent, shown in table 2, is about ¼ percentage point above the relatively small gains recorded on average since 2004. The contributions from capital deepening and MFP move up notably from the 2004-2012 pace,

---

[14]We received this projection from Dale Jorgenson by email on December 19, 2012.
[15] Although the steady-state projection does not apply to a specific time period, we think of it as pertaining to the outlook five to ten years ahead.

but these larger contributions are offset in part by the reduced contribution from labor composition.[16]

Table 2 also presents an alternative scenario that embeds a somewhat more optimistic view about the outlook for information technology. In this alternative scenario, we allow for faster MFP growth in the IT-producing sectors by setting the rate of decline in output prices in each component industry to its upper-bound value. With this change, semiconductor prices fall 6 percentage points (at an annual rate) more quickly than in the baseline, while the speedup in the other IT sectors ranges from about 1 percentage point (software) to 3¾ percentage points (computer hardware). These price changes are not especially large in the context of the observed variation since 1974 (see appendix table A1). We assume that the resulting faster diffusion of new technology boosts MFP growth in the rest of nonfarm business from the baseline value of 0.34 percent annually to the upper-bound value of 0.62 percent. All other parameters remain at their baseline values.

With these changes, steady-state growth of labor productivity rises to 2.47 percent at an annual rate, almost ¾ percentage point above the baseline estimate. The faster assumed MFP growth directly augments the rate of increase in labor productivity. It also has a multiplier effect by inducing additional capital deepening. This scenario illustrates that it would not take a very large increase in the impetus from IT to raise labor productivity growth back to the neighborhood of its long-term historical average of 2¼ percent or above.

B. Other Estimates

Table 3 compares our steady-state results to the projections of future growth in labor productivity from other analysts. The table displays the most recent projections from each

---

[16] This contribution declines not only because of the projection that educational attainment will plateau, but also because the job losses during the Great Recession were skewed toward less educated workers, which shifted the mix of employment over 2004-12 toward more skilled workers, boosting the labor composition effect over that period.

source, along with the earlier projections that were presented in OSS.[17] As shown, the earlier projections ranged from 2.0 percent to 2.5 percent at an annual rate, with an average of 2.3 percent — the same as the midpoint of the steady-state range in OSS. These earlier projections all have been revised down, some quite substantially. The average markdown from 2.3 percent to 1.9 percent virtually matches the downward revision in the steady-state estimate. Thus, compared with projections from six years ago, the average projected growth of labor productivity has moved down from about the long-run historical average to a pace somewhat below that average.

We would stress that the similarity among these projections belies the high degree of uncertainty about future productivity growth. The range of estimates from our steady-state framework hints at this uncertainty. The low end of the range (less than 1 percent) represents a dismal rate of productivity growth from a historical perspective, while the top end (about 2.8 percent) is well above the historical average. The only projection in the table with a statistically-based confidence range is that from Kahn and Rich (2013). In their regime-switching model, the 75 percent confidence band for productivity growth five years ahead runs from slightly below zero to about 4 percent. Suffice it to say, productivity growth is extremely hard to predict. Almost all analysts have failed to anticipate the major shifts in growth over the past several decades, and we should not expect better going forward.

IV. Trends in Semiconductor Technology

The contribution of information technology to economic growth depends importantly on the improvements in the semiconductor chips embedded in IT capital goods and on prices of

---

[17] With only a few exceptions, these projections refer to the nonfarm business sector as defined by BLS over horizons of ten years or more. Among the exceptions, Kahn and Rich (2013) employ a five-year horizon, while there is no explicit projection period in Fernald (2012). In addition, Fernald's projection refers to the private business sector, which includes the farm sector.

those chips. This section presents the latest available information on technological progress in the semiconductor industry and on chip prices.

A. Technology Cycles

As discussed in Aizcorbe, Oliner, and Sichel (2008), there is a broad consensus that the pace of technical advance in the semiconductor industry sped up in the mid-1990s, a development first brought to the attention of economists by Jorgenson (2001). The standard definition of a semiconductor technology cycle is the amount of time required to achieve a 30 percent reduction in the width of the smallest feature on a chip. Because chips are rectangular, a 30 percent reduction in both the horizontal and vertical directions implies about a 50 percent reduction (0.7*0.7) in the area required for the smallest chip component.

Table 4 presents the history of these scaling reductions for the semiconductor industry as a whole and microprocessor (MPU) chips produced by Intel, updating a similar table in Aizcorbe, Oliner, and Sichel (2008). As shown, the industry has achieved massive reductions in scaling over time, leaving the width of a chip component in 2012 about 450 times smaller (10,000/22) than in 1969. Except for the two-year lag at the beginning of this period, Intel always has been at the industry frontier or within a year of the frontier.[18]

Given these introduction dates, table 5 reports the average length of the technology cycle (as defined above) for various periods. For the industry as a whole, the technology cycle averaged three years until 1993 and then dropped to about two years from 1993 to 2012. Within the later period, the scaling advances were especially rapid from 1993 to 2003 and a bit slower after 2003. Even so, the average cycle since 2003 has remained substantially shorter than the

---

[18] For the 1500 nanometer process introduced in the early 1980s, the data indicate that Intel sold chips based on this technology two years before the process was used anywhere in the industry, an obvious inconsistency. Fortunately, this problem has no effect on the average length of the technology cycles that we present below because the average length depends only on the frontier technology at the beginning and end of the period under consideration, and there are no inconsistencies in these endpoint values.

three-year cycle in effect before the 1990s. For Intel's MPU chips, there has been no pullback at all from the two-year cycle. The upshot is that the cycles in semiconductor technology — a key driver of quality improvement in IT products — have remained rapid.

While the pace of miniaturization has been sustained, semiconductor producers have changed the approach used to translate these engineering gains into faster performance. Historically, each new generation of technology in semiconductors has allowed for an increase in the number of basic calculations performed per second for a given chip design. However, as speed continued to increase, dissipating the generated heat became problematic. In response, Intel shifted in 2006 toward raising "clockspeed" more slowly and boosted performance instead by placing multiple copies of the core architecture on each chip — a change enabled by smaller feature size — and by improving the design of those cores (see Shenoy and Daniel, 2006).

The effect of this strategy on the rate of increase in performance for end users has been a matter of some debate. Pillai (2013) examines the record and presents evidence that scores for Intel MPUs on benchmark performance tests—based on standard tasks designed to reflect the needs of computer users—rose more slowly from 2001 to 2008 than in the 1990s. Our own examination of more recent data suggests the slower rate of performance improvement has persisted through 2012.[19] Nonetheless, even on this slower trend, our results show that the end-user performance of Intel's MPU chips improved roughly 30 percent per year on average from 2001 to 2012. End users have continued to see substantial gains in performance, just not the extraordinary rate of increase recorded in the 1990s.

---

[19] We used SPEC performance data for this analysis. We accessed the data on December 5, 2012 and used the benchmark suite SPEC® CPU2006.

B. Prices for MPUs

Advances in semiconductor technology have driven down the constant-quality prices of MPUs and other chips at a rapid rate over the past several decades.[20] These declines, in turn, have lowered the prices of computer hardware, communication equipment, and other goods in which the chips are embedded, spurring the diffusion of IT capital goods throughout the economy. Thus, semiconductor prices play a central role in our assessment of whether the IT revolution still has legs.

On this score, the recent data on MPU prices, as measured by the producer price index (PPI), are not encouraging. As shown by the solid line in figure 2, from the late 1990s — when the BLS adopted the current PPI methodology — to 2007, MPU prices fell at an average annual rate of about 50 percent. But the rate of decline slowed in each year after 2007, so much so that the price index barely fell at all in 2012. The PPI data, if correct, would indicate that a fundamentally adverse shift in semiconductor price trends has taken place over the past several years.

In a separate in-progress paper, we are developing a new hedonic price index for MPUs, and some key results from that paper are reported here. We compiled wholesale price lists for Intel MPUs and matched these prices to benchmark performance scores and other chip characteristics.[21] We then estimated a hedonic regression back to 2006 using only the list price at the time of introduction. We omitted the list prices for subsequent periods because in many cases those prices were not adjusted down when a more powerful, closely-related chip entered

---

[20] Chips other than MPUs and memory (including those used in smartphones) are often produced using a technology behind the frontier. These chips adopt new technology, albeit with a lag. This process transmits the price declines at the frontier to a wide range of different chips.

[21] Although we do not have access to BLS' source data, comments by BLS staff indicate that published wholesale price lists for MPUs have been used to supplement the data collected by the PPI survey (Holdway, 2001). We focus on Intel because of its large share of domestic MPU production.

the market, contrary to the pattern in earlier years. The absence of price adjustment raises concern that existing chips are being sold at a discount relative to the constant list price that widens when new models are introduced. Thus, to the extent that significant chip sales are taking place at transaction prices that fall ever further below the list prices, a standard procedure that relied on those list prices or other similar prices reported by manufacturers would be biased. Our hedonic index, which only uses prices at the time of each new chip's introduction, provides a very rough way of avoiding this potential bias. This new hedonic index was incorporated into the Federal Reserve's March 2013 annual revision of its industrial production indexes.[22]

The key result from this new price index is that MPU prices have remained on a fairly steep downtrend, in sharp contrast to the picture painted by the PPI. The dashed line in figure 2 presents the MPU price index constructed by Federal Reserve staff from its inception in 1992 through 2011, the final year that incorporates the new hedonic results. The Fed index of MPU prices fell at an average annual rate of 36 percent from 2006 to 2011, somewhat less than that observed during the period of extraordinary productivity gains in the late 1990s, but substantially greater than the drop in the PPI in recent years. Moreover, unlike the PPI, the Fed's index provides no sign of a trend toward slower price declines over the past several years. All in all, the Fed's MPU price index lines up reasonably well with the MPU performance data described above — both series have reverted to historically normal rates of change after a period of unusually rapid performance gains and price declines.

---

[22] For additional information, see the discussion of the revision at http://www.federalreserve.gov/releases/g17/revisions/Current/DefaultRev.htm. The price index is available at http://www.federalreserve.gov/releases/g17/download.htm.

V. Other IT-Related Measurement Issues

Beginning in the 1970s, many studies of semiconductors, computers, communication equipment, and software have concluded that quality-adjusted IT prices have fallen at remarkable rates, and indexes capturing these price declines have been incorporated into the NIPAs in many cases (see Wasshausen and Moulton, 2006). However, despite this considerable progress on measuring IT prices, some important measurement challenges remain to be addressed. Here, we list three rather different areas that, in our view, would benefit from additional research.

First, investment in software is the largest component of IT investment, and quality adjustment has proven difficult for this category. While the BEA has closely studied software prices, this area has proved a tough nut to crack, and the agency is still using proxies for the prices of a significant fraction of software. With these proxies, the BEA's prices for own-account and custom software have increased in recent years. For prepackaged software, Copeland (2013) finds sizable declines in quality adjusted prices using scanner data.[23] Those declines are faster than those in the PPI for prepackaged software and contrast sharply with the price increases for custom and own-account software, suggesting that further work on software prices would be valuable.

Second, even if well-constructed price indexes for all IT equipment and software were available, the impact of the IT revolution may be understated for a very different reason. It has become common for U.S. manufacturing firms to outsource fabrication of electronics, frequently to offshore locations, but to retain the design and management tasks within the company, often in domestic locations. Because these so-called "factoryless manufacturers" may create the intellectual property and bear the entrepreneurial risk for products with rapidly increasing

---

[23] Also, see Prud'homme, Sanga, and Yu (2005) for similar evidence using Canadian scanner data.

quality, the real value-added of these establishments arguably should reflect the innovation embodied in the product. Because in practice this activity is often classified within wholesale trade, the resulting output does not get counted as part of the IT sector of the economy. Studies of companies using the factoryless business model indicate this may be an appreciable share of economic activity (see Bayard, Byrne, and Smith, 2013, and Doherty, 2013).

Finally, IT as defined in this paper does not encompass all products with significant electronic content. We expect the prices for a broad array of electronic equipment would reflect the price declines for their semiconductor inputs, including navigation equipment, electromedical equipment, and a variety of types of industrial process equipment.[24] In fact, the PPIs for the output of these industries increase in most cases, again raising an important question for price analysts to investigate.[25]

These three rather different concerns all point to the possibility that the full impact of the IT revolution has not yet been recorded.

VI. Conclusions

Is the information technology revolution over? In light of the slower pace of productivity gains since the mid-2000s, Robert Gordon has argued that the boost to productivity growth from adoption of IT largely had run its course by that point. Erik Brynjolfsson and others make the opposite case, arguing that dramatic transformations related to IT continue and will leave a significant imprint on economic activity. We bring three types of evidence to this debate, focusing on the IT capital that underlies IT-related innovations in the economy.

---

[24] Even products within the IT category may benefit from a closer look. For example, Chwelos, Berndt, and Cockburn (2008) develop hedonic price indexes for personal digital assistants from 1999 to 2004, and they find average price declines ranging from 19 to 26 percent per year.
[25] A BLS paper on the use of hedonics (Holdway, 2011) indicates that resource constraints have limited the expansion of the use of hedonic techniques.

What does this evidence show? Our analysis indicates that the contributions of IT to labor productivity growth from 2004 to 2012 look much as they did before 1995, supporting Gordon's side of the argument. Our baseline projection of the trend in labor productivity points to moderate growth, better than the average pace from 2004 to 2012, but still noticeably below the very long-run average rate of labor productivity growth. On the more optimistic side, we present evidence that innovation for semiconductors is continuing at a rapid pace, raising the possibility of a second wave in the IT revolution, and we see a reasonable prospect that the pace of labor productivity growth could rise to its long-run average of 2¼ percent or even above. Accordingly, with all the humility that must attend any projection of labor productivity, our answer to the title question of the paper is: No, the information technology revolution is not over.

Table 1. Contributions to Growth of Labor Productivity in the Nonfarm Business Sector[a]

	1974-1995 (1)	1995-2004 (2)	2004-2012 (3)	Change at 1995 (2) – (1)	Change at 2004 (3) – (2)
1. Growth of labor productivity[b]	1.56	3.06	1.56	1.50	-1.50
Contributions (percentage points per year):					
2. Capital deepening	.74	1.22	.74	.48	-.48
3. IT capital	.41	.78	.36	.37	-.42
4. Computer hardware	.18	.38	.12	.20	-.26
5. Software	.16	.27	.16	.11	-.11
6. Communication equipment	.07	.13	.08	.06	-.05
7. Other capital	.33	.44	.38	.11	-.06
8. Labor composition	.26	.22	.34	-.04	.12
9. Multifactor productivity (MFP)	.56	1.62	.48	1.06	-1.14
10. Effect of adjustment costs	.07	.07	-.02	.00	-.09
11. Effect of utilization	-.01	-.06	.16	-.05	.22
12. MFP after adjustments	.50	1.61	.34	1.11	-1.27
13. IT-producing sectors	.36	.72	.28	.36	-.44
14. Semiconductors	.09	.37	.14	.28	-.23
15. Computer hardware	.17	.17	.04	.00	-.13
16. Software	.06	.10	.08	.04	-.02
17. Communication equipment	.05	.07	.02	.02	-.05
18. Other nonfarm business	.13	.90	.06	.77	-.84
Memo:					
19. Total IT contribution[c]	.77	1.50	.64	.73	-.86

Source. Authors' calculations.
a. Detail may not sum to totals due to rounding.
b. Measured as 100 times average annual log difference for the indicated years.
c. Sum of lines 3 and 13.

Table 2. Steady-State Growth of Labor Productivity in the Nonfarm Business Sector[a]

Source	History 2004-12	Steady State Baseline[b]	Steady State Alternative[c]
Growth of labor productivity (percent per year)	1.56	1.80	2.47
Contributions (percentage points):			
Capital deepening	.74	1.03	1.34
Change in labor composition	.34	.07	.07
MFP	.48	.70	1.06
IT-producing sectors[d]	.28	.38	.46
Other nonfarm business[d,e]	.06	.33	.60
Adjustments[f]	.14	.00	.00
Memo:			
MFP growth in other nonfarm business	.06	.34	.62

Sources. Authors' estimates.
a. Detail may not sum to totals due to rounding.
b. Uses midpoint values for all parameters.
c. Uses upper-bound values for decline in IT-sector prices and upper-bound value for MFP growth in other nonfarm business. All other parameters set to midpoint values.
d. After excluding the effects of adjustment costs and cyclical utilization.
e. Equals the product of MFP growth in this sector (shown in the memo line) and the sector's share of nonfarm business output (which is close to one).
f. For effects of adjustment costs and cyclical utilization.

Table 3. Alternative Projections of Growth of Labor Productivity
(Percent per year)

Source	As of	
	2007	2012-13
1. Baseline steady-state estimate	2.3	1.8
2. Congressional Budget Office	2.3	2.1
3. John Fernald	n.a.	1.9
4. Robert Gordon	2.0	1.55[26]
5. James Kahn and Robert Rich	2.5	1.8
6. Survey of Professional Forecasters[a]	2.2	1.8
Average of lines 2 through 6	*2.3*	*1.9*

Sources. 2007 estimates from Oliner, Sichel, and Stiroh (2007), table 12. 2012-13 estimates from Congressional Budget Office (2013), table 2-2; Fernald (2012), "Benchmark Scenario" in table 2; Gordon (2010), with adjustment provided in private correspondence; Kahn-Rich Productivity Model Update (February 2013), posted at http://www.newyorkfed.org/research/national_economy/richkahn_prodmod.pdf; Federal Reserve Bank of Philadelphia, *Survey of Professional Forecasters*, February 15, 2013, table 7.
a. Median forecast in the survey.

---

[26] We have adjusted this forecast to reflect a correction received from Robert Gordon after the publication of this paper in The International Productivity Monitor, posted at http://www.csls.ca/ipm/25/IPM-25-Byrne-Oliner-Sichel.pdf.

Table 4. Year of Introduction for New Semiconductor Technology

Process (nanometers)	Industry Frontier	Intel MPU Chips
10,000	1969	1971
8000	1972	n.a.
6000	n.a.	1974
5000	1974	n.a.
4000	1976	n.a.
3000	1979	1979[a]
2000	1982	n.a.
1500	1984	1982
1250	1986	n.a.
1000	1988	1989
800	1990	1991
600	1993	1994
350	1995	1995
250	1997	1997
180	1999	1999
130	2001	2001
90	2003	2004
65	2005	2005
45	2007	2007
32	2010	2010
22	2012	2012

Source. Industry frontier: VLSI Research Inc. (2006) for the 65 nanometer and earlier processes and private correspondence with Dan Hutcheson (November 10, 2012) for the more recent processes. Intel MPU chips: http://www.intel.com/pressroom/kits/quickreffam.htm.
a. Intel began making MPU chips with this process in 1979. We omitted Intel's earlier use of the 3000 nanometer process (starting in 1976) to produce less complex devices, such as scales.
n.a.: Not available.

Table 5. Semiconductor Technology Cycles
(Years needed for 30 percent reduction in linear scaling)

Industry Frontier		Intel MPU Chips	
Period	Years	Period	Years
1969-1993	3.0	1971-1994	2.9
1993-2012	2.1	1994-2012	1.9
1993-2003	1.9	1994-2004	1.9
2003-2012	2.3	2004-2012	2.0

Source: Authors' calculations from data in table 4.

Figure 1. Current-dollar Output Shares for IT Industries

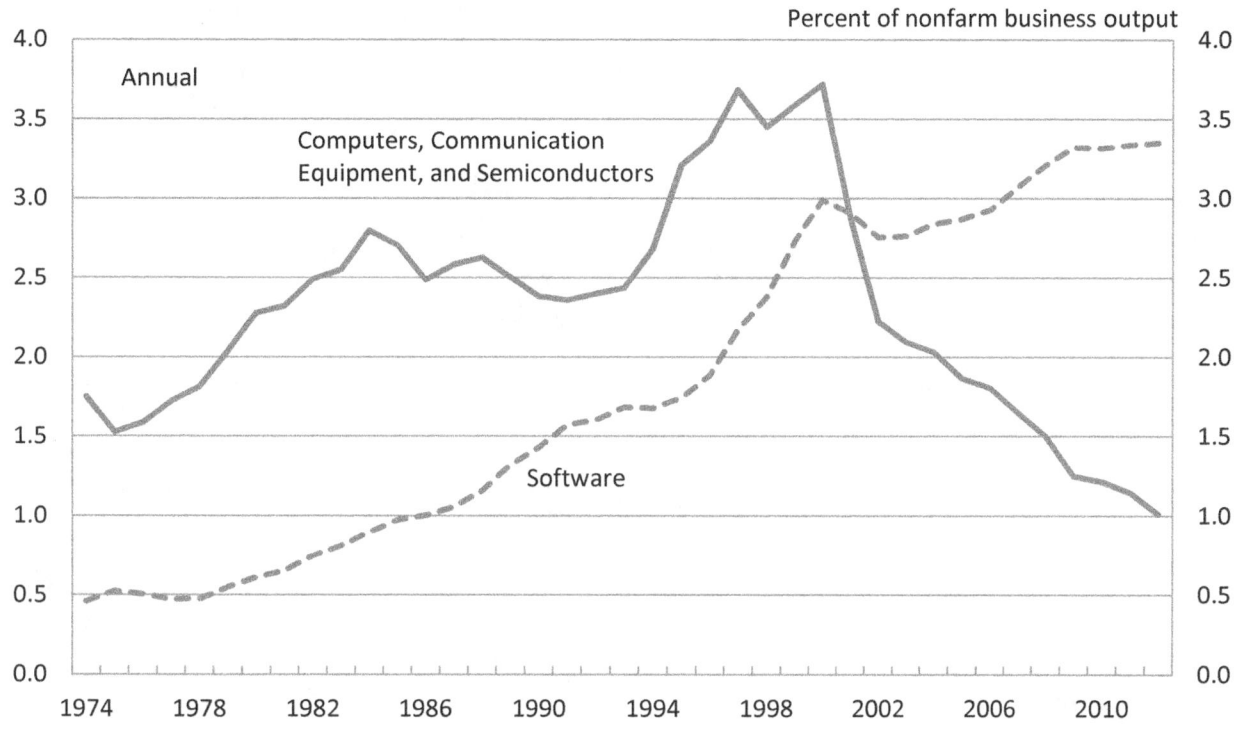

Source. Authors' calculations.

Figure 2. Price Indexes for Microprocessors (MPUs)

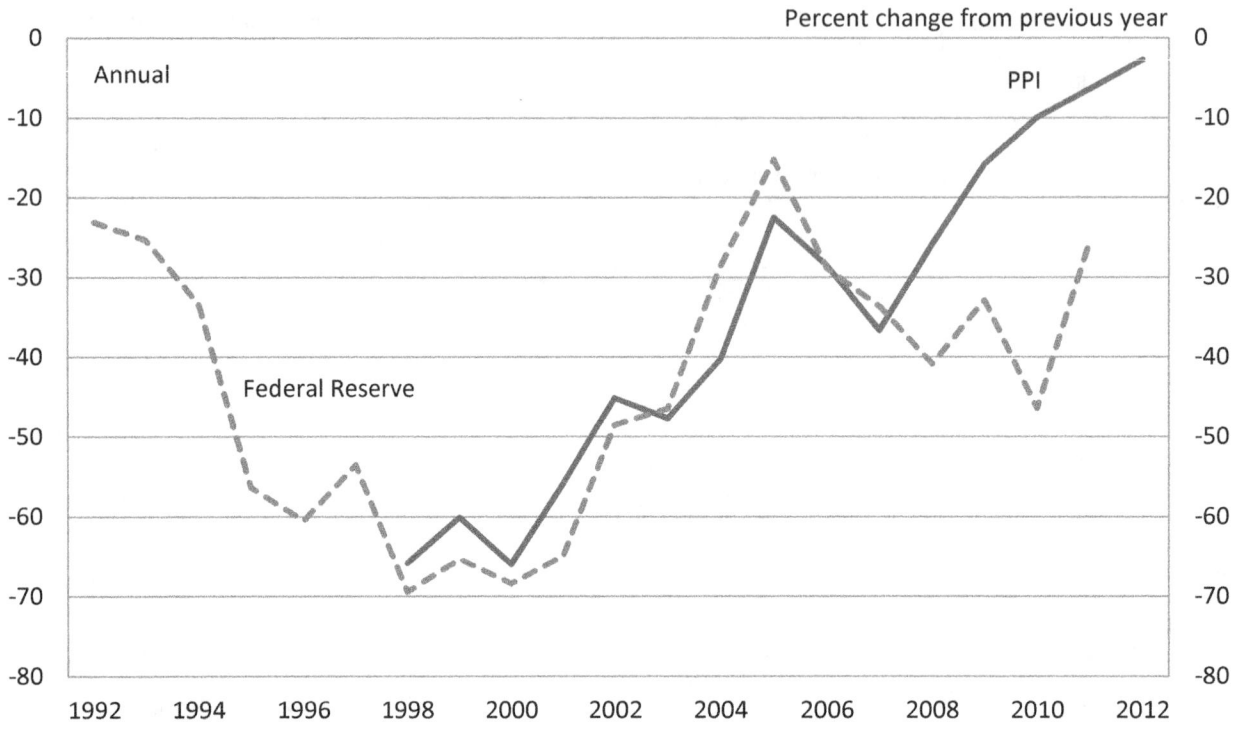

Source. BLS and Federal Reserve Board

References

Aizcorbe, Ana, Stephen D. Oliner, and Daniel E. Sichel. 2008. "Shifting Trends in Semiconductor Prices and the Pace of Technological Progress." *Business Economics* 43(3): 23-39.

Baily, Martin Neil, James L. Manyika, and Shalabh Gupta. 2013. "U.S. Productivity Growth: An Optimistic Perspective." *International Productivity Monitor*, no. 25, Spring.

Basu, Susanto, John G. Fernald, and Matthew D. Shapiro. 2001. "Productivity Growth in the 1990s: Technology, Utilization, or Adjustment?" *Carnegie-Rochester Series on Public Policy* 55: 117-65.

Bayard, Kimberly, David Byrne, and Dominic Smith. 2013. "The Scope of U.S. Factoryless Manufacturing." Available at http://www.upjohn.org/MEG/papers/baybyrsmi.pdf.

Brynjolfsson, Erik, and Andrew McAfee. 2011. *Race Against the Machine: How the Digital Revolution is Accelerating Innovation, Driving Productivity, and Irreversibly Transforming Employment and the Economy.* Digital Frontier Press.

Byrne, David, and Carol Corrado. 2007. "Prices for Communications Equipment: Rewriting a 46-Year Record." National Bureau of Economic Research conference paper, July.

Chwelos, P.D., Ernst. R. Berndt, and Iain M. Cockburn. 2008. "Faster, Smaller, Cheaper: An Hedonic Price Analysis of PDAs." *Applied Economics* 40: 2839-56.

Congressional Budget Office. 2013. *The Budget and Economic Outlook: Fiscal Years 2013 to 2023.* Washington (August). Available at http://www.cbo.gov/sites/default/files/cbofiles/attachments/43907-BudgetOutlook.pdf.

Copeland, Adam. 2013. "Seasonality, Consumer Heterogeneity and Price Indexes: the Case of Prepackaged Software." *Journal of Productivity Analysis* 39: 47-59.

Corrado, Carol, Jonathan Haskel, Cecilia Jona-Lasinio, and Massimiliano Iommi. 2012. "Intangible Capital and Growth in Advanced Economies: Measurement Methods and Comparative Results." IZA Discussion Paper No. 6733, July.

Corrado, Carol, and Charles Hulten. 2012. "Innovation Accounting." The Conference Board, Economics Program Working Paper No. 12-04, October.

Corrado, Carol, Charles Hulten, and Daniel Sichel. 2009. "Intangible Capital and U.S. Economic Growth." *Review of Income and Wealth* 55(3): 661-85.

Cowen, Tyler. 2011. *The Great Stagnation: How America Ate All the Low-Hanging Fruit of Modern History, Got Sick, and Will (Eventually) Feel Better Again.* Dutton.

Doherty, Maureen. 2013. "Reflecting Factoryless Goods Production in the U.S. Statistical System." Available at http://www.upjohn.org/MEG/papers/Doherty_Reflecting%20Factoryless%20GoodsProduction.pdf.

Feenstra, Robert C., Benjamin R. Mandel, Marshall B. Reinsdorf, and Matthew J. Slaughter. 2013. "Effects of Terms of Trade Gains and Tariff Changes on the Measurement of U.S. Productivity Growth." *American Economic Journal: Economic Policy* 5(1): 59-93.

Fernald, John. 2012. "Productivity and Potential Output before, during, and after the Great Recession." Federal Reserve Bank of San Francisco Working Paper 2012-18. Available at http://www.frbsf.org/publications/economics/papers/2012/wp12-18bk.pdf.

Flamm, Kenneth. 2007. "The Microeconomics of Microprocessor Innovation." National Bureau of Economic Research conference paper, July.

Gordon, Robert J. 2013. "U.S. Productivity Growth: The Slowdown Has Returned After a Temporary Revival." *International Productivity Monitor*, no. 25, Spring.

Gordon, Robert J. 2012. "Is U.S. Economic Growth Over? Faltering Innovation Confronts the Six Headwinds." NBER Working Paper No. 18315. Available at http://www.nber.org/papers/w18315.

Gordon, Robert J. 2010. "Revisiting U.S. Productivity Growth over the Past Century with a View of the Future." NBER Working Paper No. 15834. Available at http://www.nber.org/papers/w15834.

Grimm, Bruce. 1998. "Price Indexes for Selected Semiconductors, 1974-96." *Survey of Current Business* 78 (February): 8-24.

Holdway, Michael. 2011. "Hedonic Methods in the Producer Price Index." Available at http://www.bls.gov/ppi/ppicomqa.htm.

Holdway, Michael. 2001. "An Alternative Methodology: Valuing Quality Change for Microprocessors in the PPI." Unpublished paper presented at Issues in Measuring Price Change and Consumption Conference, Bureau of Labor Statistics, Washington DC, June 5-8, 2000. Revised January 2001.

Jorgenson, Dale W. 2012. "A Prototype Industry-Level Production Account for the United States, 1947-2010." Presentation at the WIOD Conference, Groningen, The Netherlands, April 25.

Jorgenson, Dale W. 2001. "Information Technology and the U.S. Economy." *American Economic Review* 91(1): 1-32.

Jorgenson, Dale W., Mun S. Ho, and Kevin Stiroh. 2005. *Productivity: Information Technology and the American Growth Resurgence (volume 3)*. MIT Press.

Kahn, James A., and Robert W. Rich. 2013. Update to "Tracking Productivity in Real Time," *Current Issues in Economics and Finance* 12(8), November 2006. Federal Reserve Bank of New York. Available at http://www.newyorkfed.org/research/national_economy/richkahn_prodmod.pdf.

Kendrick, John W. 1961. *Productivity Trends in the United States*. National Bureau of Economic Research. Princeton University Press. Available at http://www.nber.org/books/kend61-1.

Oliner, Stephen D., and Daniel E. Sichel. 2002. "Information Technology and Productivity: Where Are We Now and Where Are We Going?" Federal Reserve Bank of Atlanta *Economic Review* 87 (Third Quarter): 15-44.

Oliner, Stephen D., and Daniel E. Sichel. 2000. "The Resurgence of Growth in the Late 1990s: Is Information Technology the Story?" *Journal of Economic Perspectives* 14 (Fall): 3-22.

Oliner, Stephen D., and Daniel E. Sichel. 1994. "Computers and Output Growth Revisited: How Big is the Puzzle?" *Brookings Papers on Economic Activity* 1994(2): 273-334.

Oliner, Stephen D., Daniel E. Sichel, and Kevin J. Stiroh. 2007. "Explaining a Productive Decade." *Brookings Papers on Economic Activity* 2007(1): 81-152. Appendix available at http://www.federalreserve.gov/pubs/feds/2007/200763/200763pap.pdf.

Pillai, Unni. 2013. "A Model of Technological Progress in the Microprocessor Industry". Forthcoming in *Journal of Industrial Economics*. Available at http://papers.ssrn.com/sol3/papers.cfm?abstract_id=1873992.

Prud'homme, Marc, Dimitri Sanga, and Kam Yu. 2005. "A Computer Software Price Index Using Scanner Data." *Canadian Journal of Economics* 38(3): 999-1017.

Reinhart, Carmen M., and Kenneth S. Rogoff. 2009. *This Time is Different: Eight Centuries of Financial Folly*. Princeton University Press.

Shenoy, Sunil R., and Akhilesh Daniel. 2006. "Intel Architecture and Silicon Cadence: The Catalyst for Industry Innovation." Intel white paper.

VSLI Research Inc. (2006). "Did Acceleration from a Three to Two Year Node Life Really Occur?" *The Chip Insider*, April 6.

Wasshausen, Dave, and Brent R. Moulton. 2006. "The Role of Hedonic Methods in Measuring Real GDP in the United States." Available at http://bea.gov/papers/pdf/hedonicGDP.pdf.

DATA APPENDIX

This appendix describes the data series used in the paper. All data are annual and cover the period from 1974 to 2012.

Real Output per Hour in the Nonfarm Business Sector (*Y/H*)

Data from 1974 through 2008 are from the tables the BLS makes available with its multifactor productivity (MFP) release. We used the version of the MFP data released on March 21, 2012.[27] For 2009-2012, we extended the BLS series using the annual growth rate of BLS' series for output per hour in the nonfarm business sector from its quarterly Productivity and Cost (P&C) Release.[28] We used data from the P&C release starting in 2009 so as to incorporate revisions to real output in the nonfarm business sector in the BEA's 2012 annual revision of the National Income and Product Accounts (NIPAs).

Real Output (*Y*), Current-dollar Output (*pY*), and Price Index (*p*) for the Nonfarm Business Sector

Data for real output and current-dollar output for 1974-2008 are from the MFP dataset. For 2009-2012 we extended the BLS series using annual growth rates for real output and current-dollar output in the nonfarm business sector from the NIPAs.[29] We measured *p* as an implicit price deflator, constructed as the ratio of current-dollar nonfarm business output to real nonfarm business output from the MFP dataset for the period 1974-2008. For 2009-2012, we extended the series for *p* using annual growth rates constructed from the NIPA data on real output and current-dollar output in the nonfarm business sector.

---

[27] All other series we use from the MFP data are also from that release. These data are available at http://www.bls.gov/mfp/mprdload.htm. See the spreadsheets titled "Historical Multifactor Productivity Measures (SIC 1948-87 linked to NAICS 1987-2011)" and "Information Capital by Asset Type for Major Sectors."

[28] We used data from the release dated February 7, 2013.

[29] All of the NIPA data we use are from the release dated January 30, 2013.

Labor Hours (*H*)

For 1974 to 2010, labor hours are from the MFP dataset. We extended the data to 2012 using the growth rate in hours of all persons in the nonfarm business sector from the P&C release.

Contribution of Capital Deepening in the Nonfarm Business Sector

Overall Capital Deepening

For 1974 to 2010, the contribution of overall capital deepening to growth in labor productivity is calculated as the product of: 1) the log difference of the capital-hours ratio (using real capital input) and 2) capital's income share. Our income shares are time varying and not period averages.[30] The data for the capital-hours ratio and the income shares are from the MFP dataset.

For 2011 and 2012, we extended the series for the overall capital deepening contribution using the following steps. First, we calculated the contributions from 2010 to 2012 for equipment, nonresidential structures, inventories, tenant-occupied rental housing, and land. (We use these categories because these are the ones for which the BLS makes data readily available on their website.) For each asset type, the contribution is calculated as the product of the income share and the log difference of the capital-hours ratio. For the numerator of the capital-hours ratio, we constructed productive capital stocks as described below. For the denominator, we used hours data from BLS as described above. Second, we summed these contributions to obtain a capital deepening contribution for overall capital for 2010 to 2012. Finally, we extrapolated forward from BLS' 2010 contribution with the first-difference in our calculated contributions

---

[30] For each year, the share used is the average of the income share for that year and the income share for the previous year. We use the same procedure for the IT capital shares described below.

between 2010 and 2011 and then between 2011 and 2012. We did not use the levels for 2011 and 2012 directly because we are working at a higher level of aggregation than BLS used to calculate the overall capital deepening contribution through 2010, which introduces a wedge between the results in levels for a given year.

IT Capital Deepening

For 1987 to 2010, capital deepening contributions for each type of IT capital are calculated as the product of: 1) the log difference of the capital-hours ratio using real capital input for each type of IT (computer hardware, software, and communication equipment) and 2) the income share for that type of capital. The data for capital input, hours, and the income shares for each type of IT capital are from the MFP dataset.

For 2011 to 2012, we extended the series for the contributions using a procedure exactly parallel to that for the components of overall capital deepening.

For 1974 to 1986, the BLS does not make available the needed IT detail on their website. Accordingly, for each type of IT capital, we construct contributions from data for the income share, capital input, and hours, extrapolating back from the 1987 contributions by splicing in values for these variables from the dataset we constructed for Oliner, Sichel, and Stiroh (2007).

Capital Deepening for Non-IT Assets

These contributions are calculated by subtracting the IT capital deepening contributions from the overall capital deepening contribution.

Productive Stocks

To extend the capital deepening contributions to 2011 and 2012 as described above, we used productive capital stocks to measure capital input for each category of capital, in accord with BLS methodology. For the calculations for total capital, we need productive stocks for each of the capital categories we use to sum up to total capital (equipment, nonresidential structures, inventories, tenant-occupied rental housing, and land). For the calculations for IT capital, we need productive stocks for each of the IT capital categories (computer hardware, software, and communication equipment).

Depreciable Assets

For depreciable assets (equipment and software, nonresidential structures, tenant-occupied rental housing, and the three types of IT capital) we started with productive capital stock data from the MFP dataset through 2010 (the same spreadsheets described above). We extended these BLS productive stock series to 2011 and 2012 using the perpetual inventory method with the following equation:

$$K_t = f_t\, K_{t-1} + (I_t + I_{t-1})/2,$$

where (following BLS methodology) K_t is measured as the average of the stocks at the end of years t and $t-1$. For the investment series (I_t), we started with the series for gross investment through 2010 for each category from the BLS datasets. We extended these investment series to 2011 and 2012 using growth rates of real investment for the corresponding series from the NIPAs. The term f_t is a translation factor that converts the productive stock from period $t-1$ into the productive stock for period t. We obtain this translation factor (f_t) for each period up through 2010 using the published BLS data and solving for f_t for each year in the equation above. We then use the 2010 value of f_t to generate estimates of the productive stock for 2011 and 2012.

Non-Depreciable Assets (Inventories and Land)

To extend the stock of inventories to 2011, we take the productive stock in 2010 and add the NIPA value for the change in real private inventories for 2011. Then, to extend forward to 2012, we add the 2012 value of the change in inventories to the estimated 2011 stock.

To extend the stock of land to 2011 and 2012, we assume that the real productive stock of land in 2011 and 2012 changed at the average annual rate from 2007 to 2010.

Labor Composition (q)

BLS measures the change in labor composition as the difference between the growth rate of labor input and that of labor hours. To calculate labor input, BLS divides the labor force into a number of age-sex-education cells, and then constructs a weighted average of growth in hours worked in each cell, with the weight for each cell equal to its share of total labor compensation. Through 2010, our measure of the change in labor composition is from the MFP dataset. For 2011 and 2012, we assumed that the change in labor composition generated a contribution of 0.25 percentage point to growth in labor productivity.

Income Shares (α_j)

Total Capital

For 1974 to 2010, the income share for total capital is from the MFP dataset. To extend this series to 2011 and 2012, we construct capital income for the five categories of total capital that BLS provides: equipment and software, nonresidential structures, inventories, tenant-occupied rental housing, and land. We sum these estimates to generate an estimate of total capital income. The share is then the ratio of this estimate of capital income to total income in the nonfarm business sector. Finally, we take this estimate of the capital income share and difference splice it to the 2010 value of the published BLS series for the capital income share to obtain estimates of the income share for 2011 and 2012. With an estimate of the income share for capital in hand, the income share for labor equals unity minus the income share for capital.

IT Capital

For 1987 to 2010, the income shares for each type of IT capital are from the MFP dataset. For 1974 to 1986, we difference splice in the income shares that we constructed for Oliner, Sichel, and Stiroh (2007). To extend the income shares for each IT asset to 2011 and 2012, we use a procedure parallel to the one described for the pieces that add up to total capital.

Capital Income

To estimate capital income for each type of capital for the extension to 2011 and 2012, we use the following equation:

$$capital\ income_j = \left[(R + \delta_j - \Pi_j)p_jK_j\right]T_j.$$

We discuss each component of this equation below. Although we have suppressed the time subscript for expositional convenience, these estimates of capital income vary from year to year. The extension from 2010 to 2011 and 2012 only requires data on the components for those years, but we compile data for each component back to 1974 because the steady-state calculations require the full history.

Depreciation Rate (δ_j)

For equipment and software, nonresidential structures, and tenant-occupied rental housing, we use depreciation rates reported in the MFP dataset through 2010. For 2011 and 2012, we use the value reported for 2010. For land and inventories, the depreciation rate is zero. For IT assets, we use a parallel procedure.

Expected Nominal Capital Gain/Loss (Π_j)

For each type of capital, we calculated Π_j as a three-year moving average of the percent change in the price of asset j (p_j). The moving average serves as a proxy for the unobserved expectation of price change. Through 2010, the p_j series are the investment price indexes from the MFP dataset. Except for land, each p_j series was extended to 2011 and 2012 using the growth rate of the corresponding series for NIPA investment prices.[31] For land, we extended prices to 2011 and 2012 using the average growth rate of land prices in the MFP dataset from 2007 to 2010.

Current-dollar Productive Capital Stock (p_jK_j)

For each asset, this series is simply the product of the real productive stock (K_j) and the asset price index (p_j), both of which are discussed above.

Tax Adjustment (T_j)

For each asset j, this adjustment is $T_j = (1 - c - \tau v)/(1 - \tau)$, where c is the rate of investment tax credit, τ is the corporate tax rate, and v is the present value of \$1 of tax depreciation allowances. We include a tax term (T_j) for each asset in the capital income and income share variables we construct. Through 2010, we construct the tax terms from the MFP dataset.[32] For 2011 and 2012, we use the 2010 value of each tax term.

---

[31] For equipment and software and nonresidential structures, we used the price series from NIPA table 5.3.4. For inventories, we used the implicit price deflator for nonfarm inventories from NIPA table 5.7.9B. For tenant-occupied rental housing, we used the price series for investment in multifamily residential structures from NIPA table 5.3.4. For each type of IT capital, we used prices from NIPA table 5.5.4.

[32] As part of the MFP dataset, under the heading "Additional Available Measures," BLS provides spreadsheets for 1987-2010 Rental Price Detail Measures by Asset Type for both manufacturing and non-manufacturing industries. To construct income shares for total capital and for IT capital, we need tax terms for computer hardware, software, communication equipment, other business fixed investment, inventories, tenant-occupied rental housing, and land. The tax terms do not vary across industries and do not vary much within asset classes. For computer hardware, we use the common tax term that applies to every type of hardware. For software, we use a weighted average of the tax term for pre-packaged software and custom software and the separate term for own-account software, with a weight of 0.60 on pre-packaged and custom. For communication equipment, inventories, and land, we use the single tax term for each asset type provided by the BLS. To construct the tax term for other business fixed investment (BFI excluding IT), we calculated a weighted average of the tax terms for equipment excluding IT assets and nonresidential structures. All types of nonresidential structures have a common tax term; for non-IT equipment, we used the tax term that applies to most types of equipment other than motor vehicles, nuclear fuel or IT assets. The weights are year-by-year nominal productive capital shares for equipment excluding IT assets and nonresidential structures.

Nominal Net Return (R)

We calculated R as the ex post net return earned on the productive stock of equipment and nonresidential structures. Thus, we obtain R as the solution to the following equation:

$$\sum_{j=1}^{N} \left[(R + \delta_j - \Pi_j) p_j K_j \right] T_j / pY = \sum_{j=1}^{N} \alpha_j \, ,$$

where the summations are over computer hardware, software, communication equipment, and other business fixed investment. This procedure yielded an annual series for R from 1990 to 2010. (The BLS data begin in 1987 and we need three lags for the capital gain term so these estimates of R begin in 1990.) For 2011 and 2012, we estimate R as the predicted value from a regression with the following explanatory variables: a constant, two lags of R, the rate of price change for nonfarm business output, the acceleration in real nonfarm business output, the unemployment rate, and the share of corporate profits in GNP. For the period from 1974 to 1989, we difference splice in estimates of R from Oliner, Sichel, and Stiroh (2007).

Current-Dollar Output Shares (μ_C, μ_{SW}, μ_M, μ_O, μ_S)

The denominator of each output share is current-dollar nonfarm business output (pY), the data source for which was described above. Here, we focus on the measurement of current-dollar sectoral output ($p_i Y_i$ for $i = C$, SW, M, O, and S), which is the numerator in each share.

Computer Sector

For 1987 to 2011, we used Census Bureau data from the Annual Survey of Manufacturers (ASM) on product shipments of computer and peripheral equipment (NAICS category 3341). This series includes computer and peripheral equipment shipped by domestic establishments regardless of their industry classification. Before 1987, the ASM data are available only on an industry basis. Industry shipments differ from product shipments by including secondary noncomputer products shipped by establishments in the computer and peripheral equipment industry and by excluding computer and peripheral equipment shipped by establishments in other industries. Because of the resulting level difference between the two series, we extrapolate the 1987 level of ASM product shipments back in time using the annual percent changes in ASM industry shipments. For 2012, we extrapolated the 2011 level of the ASM product shipments forward using a proxy for current-dollar shipments of computer and peripheral equipment. The proxy variable is the product of the annual average level of the Federal Reserve's industrial production index for computer and peripheral equipment and the NIPA price index for all final sales of this equipment (NIPA table 1.2.4, line 17). We moved the 2011 level of ASM product shipments forward to 2012 by the percent change in the proxy series.

Software Sector

For 1995 to 2011, we used NIPA data on current-dollar final sales of software, adjusted to exclude own-account software produced by the government. The data are in supplemental NIPA tables posted at http://www.bea.gov/national/info_comm_tech.htm under the headings "GDP and Final Sales of Software" and "Software Investment and Prices, by Type". We extrapolated the 1995 level back to earlier years and the 2011 level forward to 2012 using the annual percent changes in the NIPA series for private fixed investment in software (NIPA table 1.5.5, line 33).

Communication Equipment Sector

We follow the same procedure described above for the computer sector. That is, we use ASM product shipments for communication equipment (NAICS category 3342) for 1987-2011; we then extrapolate back in time with the annual percent changes in ASM industry shipments and forward to 2012 with the percent change in a proxy series for current-dollar output of communication equipment. The proxy variable is the product of the annual average level of the Federal Reserve's industrial production index for communication equipment and a price index for domestic output of this equipment constructed using the method described in Byrne and Corrado (2007). Because the Byrne-Corrado index is not yet available for 2012, we assume the 2012 percent change equaled that for 2011.

Semiconductor Sector

Here too we rely on Census shipments data. For 1987-2011, we use ASM product shipments for integrated circuits (NAICS category 3344131). We then extrapolate back in time with the annual percent changes in ASM industry shipments for semiconductors and related devices (NAICS code 334413), the closest available industry to integrated circuits. For 2012, we extrapolate the 2011 level of the ASM product shipments forward using the annual percent change in current-dollar shipments of integrated circuits calculated by Federal Reserve staff.

Other Nonfarm Business

We estimate current-dollar output in this sector as a residual after accounting for all other components of nonfarm business output:

$$p_O Y_O = pY - p_C Y_C - p_{SW} Y_{SW} - p_M Y_M - p_S (S_x - S_m),$$

where the final term is current-dollar net exports of semiconductors. (This is the only part of semiconductor production that shows up in domestic final output.) The data sources for pY, $p_C Y_C$, $p_{SW} Y_{SW}$, and $p_M Y_M$ were described above. We obtain data on current-dollar net exports of semiconductors as follows. For 1989 to 2011, we use series constructed by Federal Reserve Board staff for current-dollar exports and imports of integrated circuits (NAICS code 3344131), which are based on data from the International Trade Commission. We extrapolate the 1989 levels for both series back to 1978 using similarly constructed series for semiconductors and related devices (NAICS code 334413). Before 1978, the detailed trade data are not available, and we extend the export and import series back in time using the annual percent change in domestic shipments of semiconductors (the series $p_S Y_S$ described above). For 2012, we extrapolate forward the 2011 levels of both exports and imports using the annual percent change in current-dollar shipments of integrated circuits calculated by Federal Reserve staff (the same series used for the 2012 value of semiconductor sector output).

Ratio of Semiconductor Output to Domestic Semiconductor Use ($1+\theta$).

Domestic semiconductor use can be expressed as domestic semiconductor output minus net exports of semiconductors. Thus,

$$1+\theta = Y_S / [Y_S - (S_x - S_m)] = p_S Y_S / [p_S Y_S - (p_S S_x - p_S S_m)],$$

where the second equality converts each series to current dollars. The data sources for $p_S Y_S$ and $p_S S_x - p_S S_m$ were described above.

Rates of Relative Price Change (π_C, π_{SW}, π_M, π_S).

Each π_i series ($i = C$, SW, M, and S) represents the rate of change in the price ratio p_i / p_O, where p_O is the price index for other nonfarm business.[33] Here, we describe the data source for each price series that enters these ratios.

Computer Sector

For 1978-2012, we measure p_C with the NIPA price index for final sales of computers and peripheral equipment (NIPA table 1.2.4, line 17). For earlier years, we extrapolate back the 1978 level with the percent change in the NIPA price index for private fixed investment in computers

---

[33] We compute the rate of change in each relative price as the percent change from the prior year's price ratio, not as a log difference. Although growth accounting studies typically use the log difference approximation to calculate rates of change, this approximation is inaccurate for percent changes as large as those observed for the relative prices of computers and semiconductors.

and peripheral equipment (NIPA table 1.5.4, line 32), trend-adjusted to decline one percentage point faster per year. This trend adjustment accounts for the difference in the average annual decline over 1978-95 between the price indexes for private fixed investment in computers and final sales of computers.

Software Sector

For 1995-2011, p_{SW} is an implicit price deflator for final sales of software excluding own-account software produced by the government. Using NIPA data, we calculate this deflator as the ratio of current-dollar final sales excluding government own-account software (the series $p_{SW}Y_{SW}$ described above) to a chain aggregate of real software outlays with the same coverage. The data for this calculation come from the supplemental NIPA tables posted at http://www.bea.gov/national/info_comm_tech.htm under the headings "GDP and Final Sales of Software" and "Software Investment and Prices, by Type". We extrapolate the 1995 level of the price deflator back in time and the 2011 level forward to 2012 with the annual percent change in the NIPA price index for private fixed investment in software (NIPA table 1.5.4, line 33). We did not use a trend adjustment because the price series for software investment fell at a similar rate on average over 1995-2011 as the price deflator for final sales of software.

Communication Equipment Sector

For 1974-2011, we measure p_M with a price index for domestic output of communication equipment constructed using the method described in Byrne and Corrado (2007). Because this index is not yet available for 2012, we assume the percent change in 2012 was the same as in 2011.

Other Final-output Sector

p_O is measured as an implicit deflator that equals the ratio of current-dollar output for this sector (the series $p_O Y_O$ defined above) to a chain aggregate of the sector's real output (Y_O). We construct Y_O by starting with our series for real nonfarm business output (Y) and then "chain stripping-out" all other components of Y (that is, real output of computers, software, and communication equipment, along with real exports and imports of semiconductors). To construct the series for real exports and imports of semiconductors needed for the chain strip-out, we assumed that the price of both exports and imports of semiconductors equals the semiconductor price series described in the next paragraph.

Semiconductor Sector

For 1977-2012, the data source for p_S is the internal Federal Reserve price index for integrated circuits (NAICS product class 3344131 back to 1992, linked to the analogous index for SIC code 36741 for 1977-92). For the years before 1977, we extrapolate back using the price index for memory chips in Grimm (1998). Because Grimm's index covers a narrower set of chips than the Federal Reserve index, we level-adjust the annual percent changes in Grimm's index by the ratio of the percent change in the Federal Reserve index to that in Grimm's index between 1977 and 1978, the earliest overlap period.

Semiconductors as a Share of Current-dollar Input Costs ($\beta_C^S, \beta_{SW}^S, \beta_M^S, \beta_O^S$)

Computer Sector

For 1997-2011, we estimate β_C^S with proprietary data from iSuppli Corp. on the annual semiconductor cost share of seven different types of computing equipment. We aggregate the product-specific cost shares with domestic shipments weights that vary from year to year. For

2012, we use the share estimated for 2011. For 1990-96, we extrapolate back the 1997 share using the annual percent changes in the estimated worldwide semiconductor share in computing equipment; we estimate these shares from a variety of proprietary data sources. Finally, for years before 1990, we set the cost share to be a shipment-weighted average of the cost shares for personal computers and all other computing equipment; in this calculation, we use the semiconductor cost shares from 1997, the earliest year for which we have the iSuppli data.

Software Sector

We set β_{SW}^{S} to zero because semiconductors are not a direct input to software production. (The software industry uses computers and communication equipment that contain semiconductors, but it does not directly use semiconductors.)

Communication Equipment Sector

For 1997-2011, we estimate β_{M}^{S} with proprietary data from iSuppli Corp. on the annual semiconductor cost share of 14 different types of communication equipment. We aggregate the product-specific cost shares with domestic shipments weights that vary from year to year. For 2012, we use the share estimated for 2011. For 1990-96, we extrapolate back the 1997 share using the annual percent changes in the estimated worldwide semiconductor share in communication equipment; we estimate these shares from a variety of proprietary data sources. Finally, for years before 1990, we extrapolate back the 1990 share using the annual percent changes in the share constructed in Oliner and Sichel (2002) using data from the Semiconductor Industry Association. See the data appendix in Oliner and Sichel (2002) for details.

Other Final-output Sector.

To estimate β_O^S, note that equation A22 in Oliner and Sichel (2002) shows that:

$$\mu_S = \sum_{i=1}^{4} \mu_i \beta_i^S (1+\theta),$$

which can be written with explicit sectoral notation as

$$\mu_S = \left[\mu_C \beta_C^S + \mu_{SW} \beta_{SW}^S + \mu_M \beta_M^S + \mu_O \beta_O^S \right](1+\theta).$$

Solving this equation for β_O^S yields

$$\beta_O^S = \frac{\mu_S - (1+\theta)[\mu_C \beta_C^S + \mu_{SW} \beta_{SW}^S + \mu_M \beta_M^S]}{\mu_O (1+\theta)}.$$

The data sources for all series on the right-hand side of this expression have been discussed

above.

Appendix Table A1. Parameter Values for Steady-State Calculations

| | Historical Averages | | | Steady-State | | Method for |
	1974-1995	1996-2004	2005-2012	Lower Bound	Upper Bound	Setting Bounds
Output shares[1] (μ)						
1. Computer hardware	1.11	1.12	.44	.15	.50	A
2. Software	1.02	2.60	3.17	3.00	3.50	A
3. Communication equipment	.85	1.08	.47	.25	.60	A
4. Other final-output sectors	97.05	95.20	95.84	96.52	95.32	B
5. Net exports of semiconductors	-.04	-.01	.08	.08	.08	C
6. Total semiconductor output	.39	.80	.52	.40	.65	A
Semiconductor cost shares[1] (β)						
7. Computer hardware	14.79	22.23	22.31	15.00	20.00	A
8. Software	.00	.00	.00	.00	.00	C
9. Communication equipment	6.00	17.29	18.88	14.00	20.00	A
10. Other final-output sectors	.21	.38	.26	.29	.34	B
Relative inflation rates[2] (π)						
11. Semiconductors	-26.25	-43.29	-26.28	-24.23	-36.35	D
12. Computer hardware	-19.11	-22.58	-14.72	-15.21	-22.81	D
13. Software	-5.57	-2.81	-2.43	-3.40	-5.11	D
14. Communication equipment	-6.89	-13.31	-8.55	-7.01	-10.51	D
Depreciation rates[3] (δ)						
15. Computer hardware	23.95	28.80	31.38	31.38	31.38	C
16. Software	31.58	34.44	37.75	37.75	37.75	C
17. Communication equipment	11.76	11.20	11.79	11.79	11.79	C
18. Other business fixed capital	5.69	5.76	5.38	5.38	5.38	C
Expected capital gains/losses[4] (Π)						
19. Computer hardware	-15.69	-15.74	-9.61	-10.28	-15.42	E
20. Software	.35	-.41	-.26	-.27	-.40	E
21. Communication equipment	2.45	-3.44	-3.73	-2.86	-4.29	E
22. Other business fixed capital	5.74	3.10	2.69	2.33	3.49	E
Capital-output ratios ($Tp_K K /pY$)						
23. Computer hardware	.020	.030	.024	.020	.029	A
24. Software	.026	.068	.084	.082	.092	A
25. Communication equipment	.072	.081	.070	.060	.075	A
26. Other business fixed capital	2.32	1.91	2.09	1.90	2.30	A

(*continued*)

Appendix Table A1. Parameter Values for Steady-State Calculations (*continued*)

	Historical Averages			Steady-State		Method for
	1974-1995	1996-2004	2005-2012	Lower Bound	Upper Bound	Setting Bounds
Income shares[1] (α)						
27. Computer hardware	.98	1.50	1.13	.96	1.55	B
28. Software	1.04	2.76	3.75	3.66	4.12	B
29. Communication equipment	1.29	1.67	1.54	1.27	1.70	B
30. Other business fixed capital	19.91	16.53	19.38	18.29	19.47	B
31. Other capital[5]	8.85	7.53	8.11	8.11	8.11	C
32. Labor	67.93	70.01	66.09	67.11	65.07	B
Other parameters						
33. Growth of "other" sector MFP[3]	.14	.94	.06	.06	.62	F
34. Change in labor composition[3] (*q*)	.26	.22	.34	.00	.14	G
35. Nominal return on capital[3] (*R*)	8.62	5.99	6.58	6.58	6.58	C
36. Ratio of domestic semiconductor output to domestic use (1+θ)	.93	1.01	1.20	1.20	1.20	C

1. Current-dollar shares, in percent.
2. Output price inflation in each sector minus that in the "other final-output" sector, in percentage points.
3. In percent.
4. Three-year moving average of price inflation for each asset, in percent.
5. Includes land, inventories, and tenant-occupied housing.

Key: Methods for setting steady-state bounds.
A. Range around recent values.
B. Implied by other series.
C. Average value over 2005-2012.
D. The lower and upper bounds equal, respectively, 0.8 and 1.2 times the average rate of change over 1974-2012.
E. The lower and upper bounds equal, respectively, 0.8 and 1.2 times the average rate of change over 1996-2012.
F. The lower bound equals the average rate of MFP growth in this sector over 2005-12; the upper bound equals ⅔ times the average rate over 1996-2004.
G. Based on a forecast obtained from Dale Jorgenson for 2012-22 (private correspondence, December 19, 2012). Jorgenson's forecast is a point estimate of 0.07 percent annually. We set symmetric bounds around this point forecast.